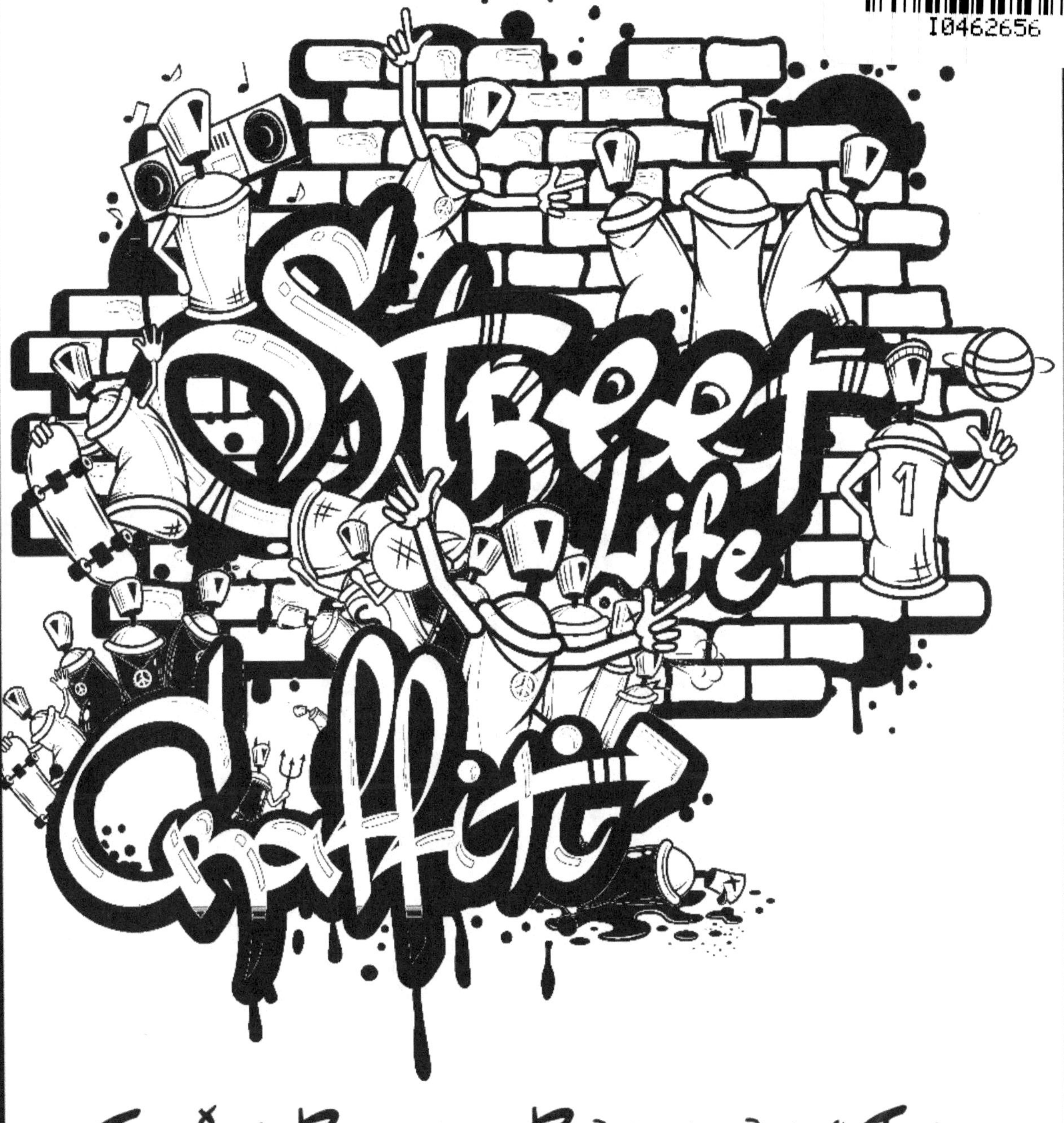

THIS BOOK BELONGS TO:

____

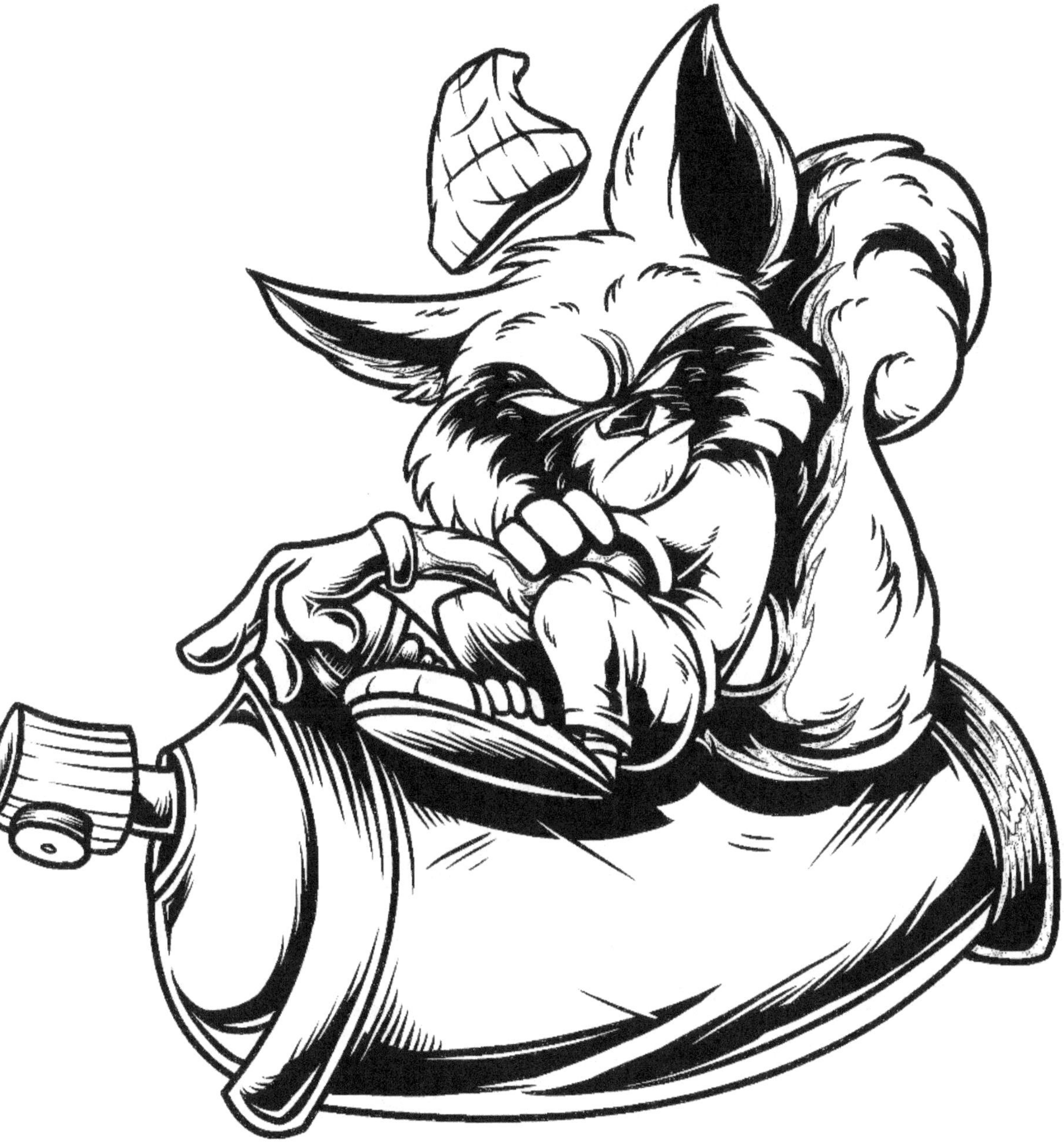

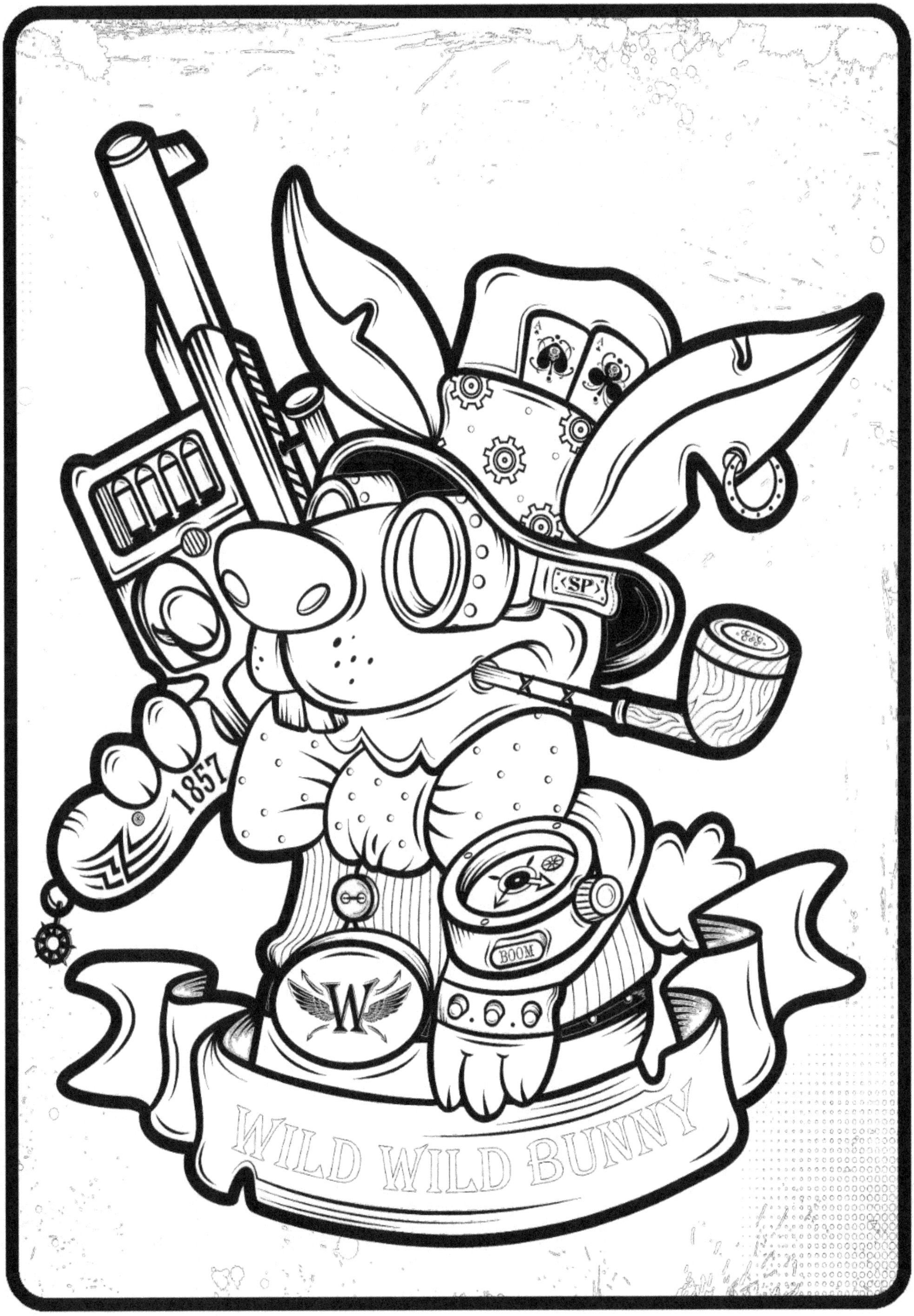

SP
1857
BOOM
W
WILD WILD BUNNY

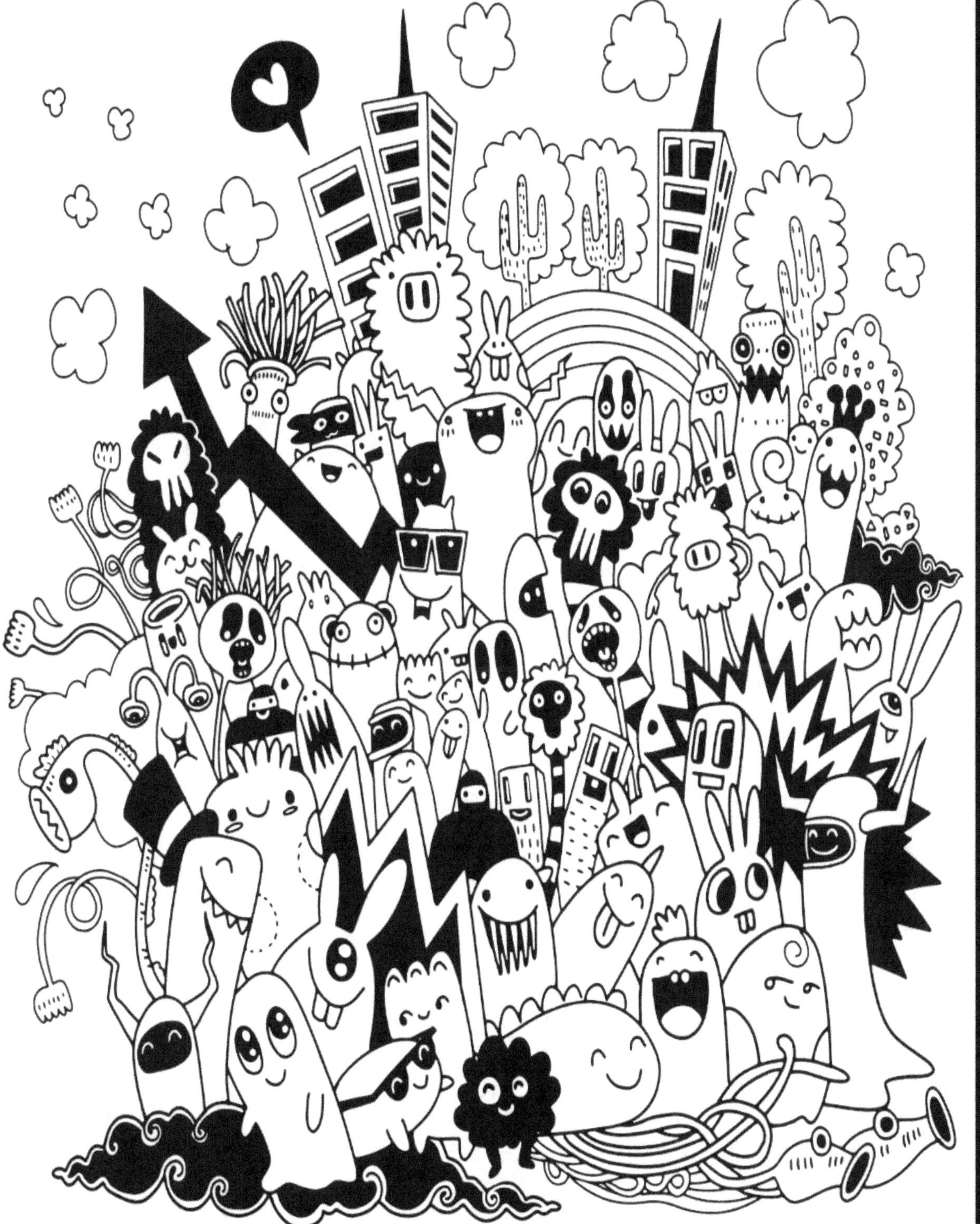

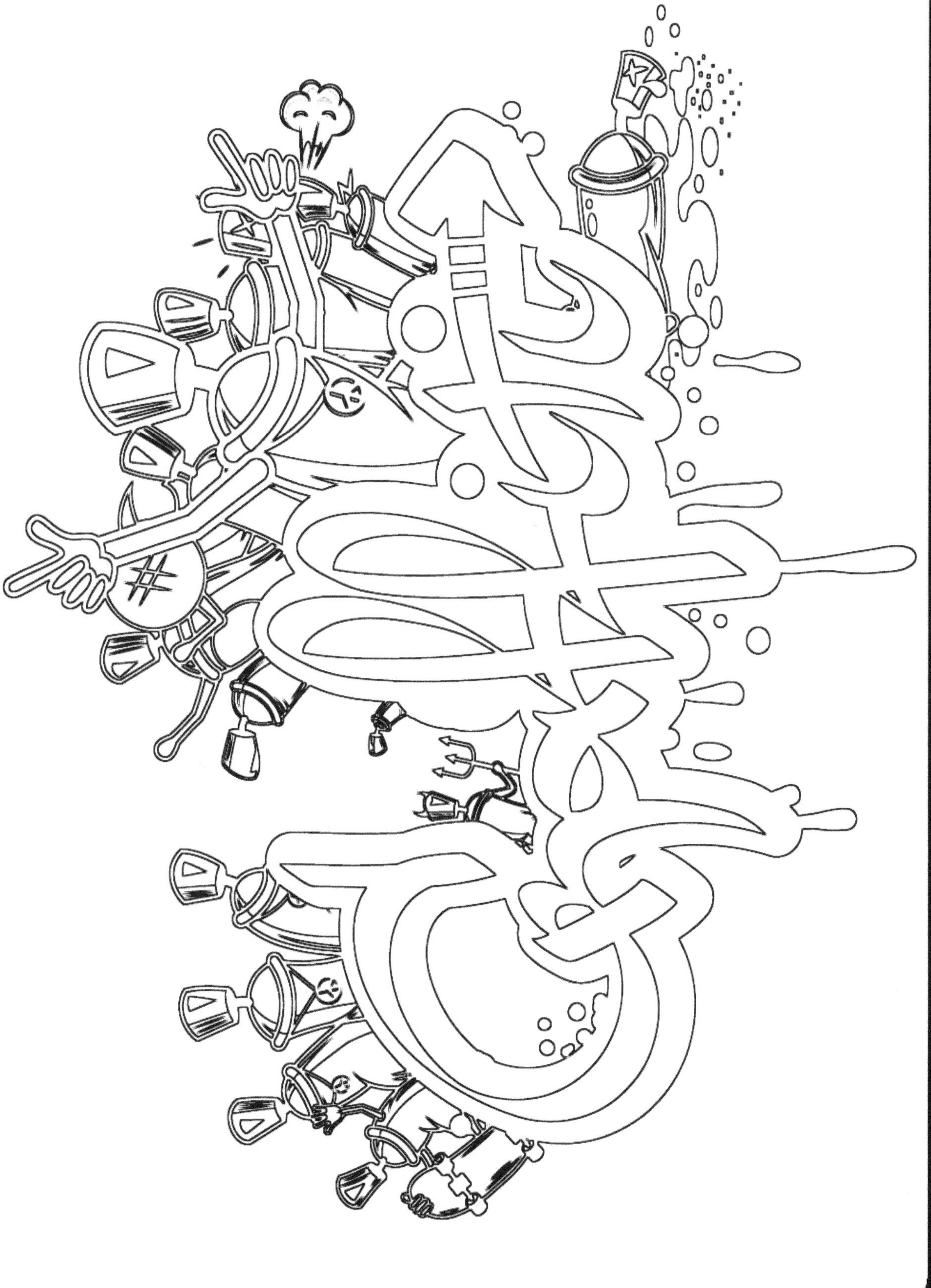

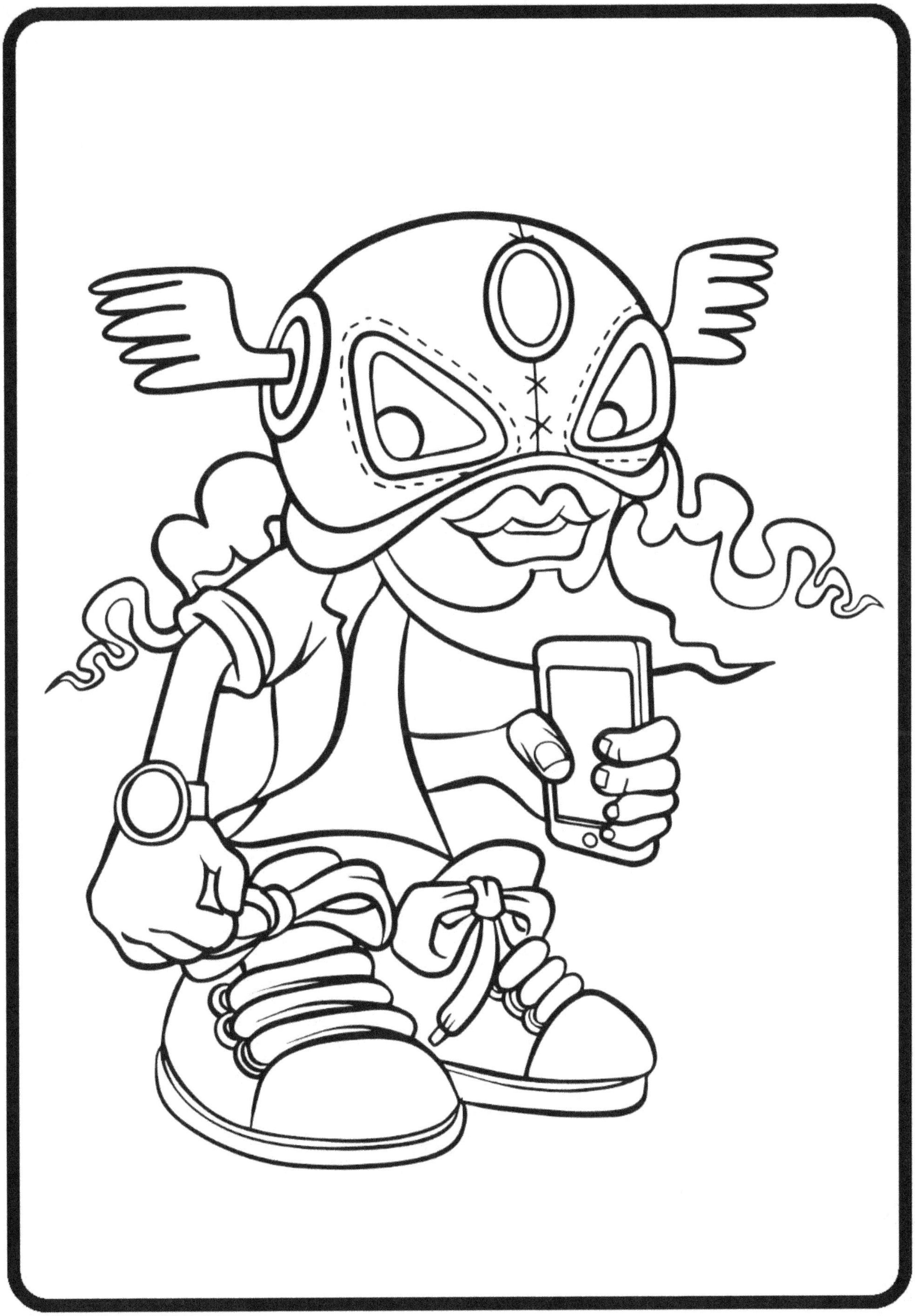

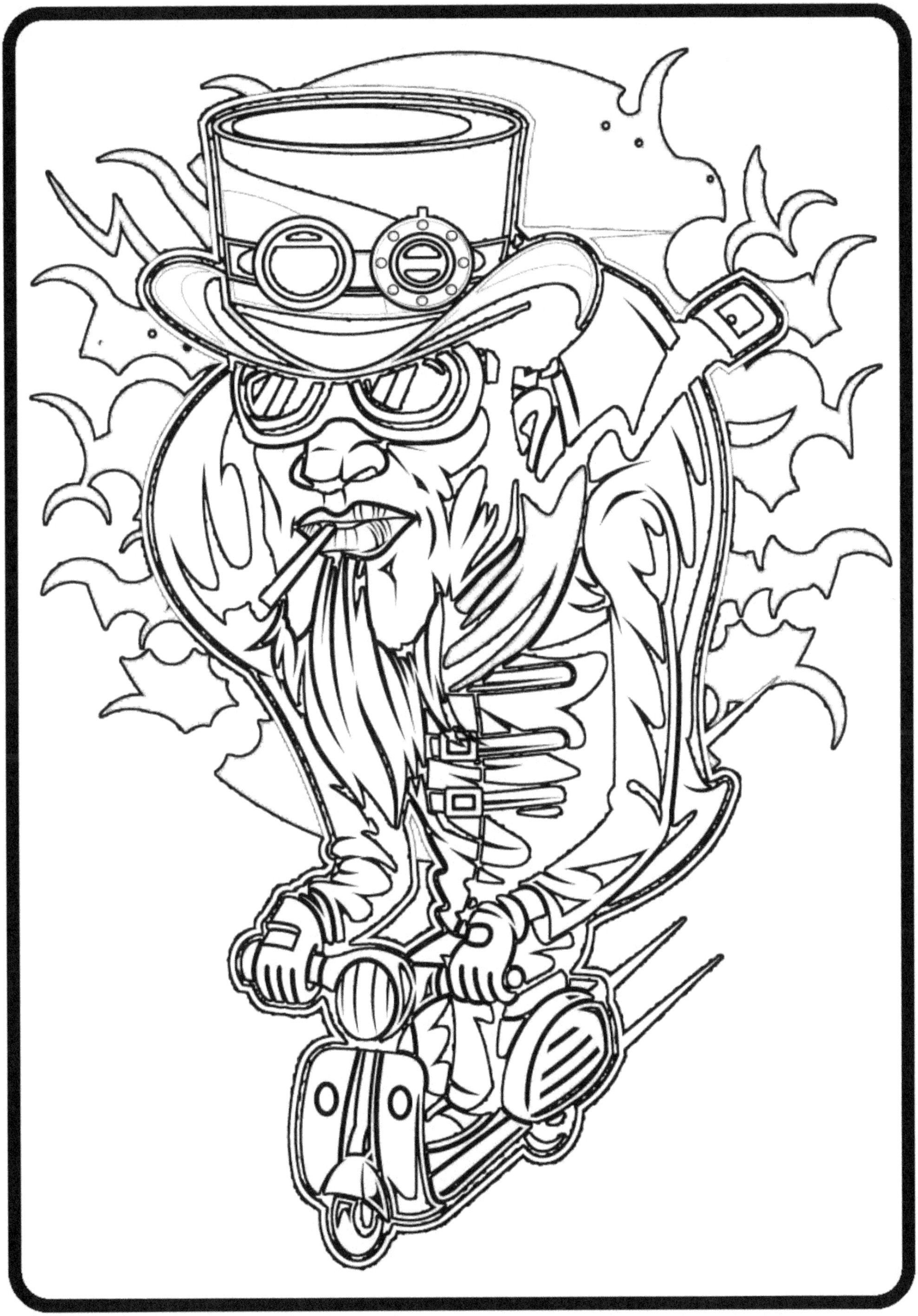

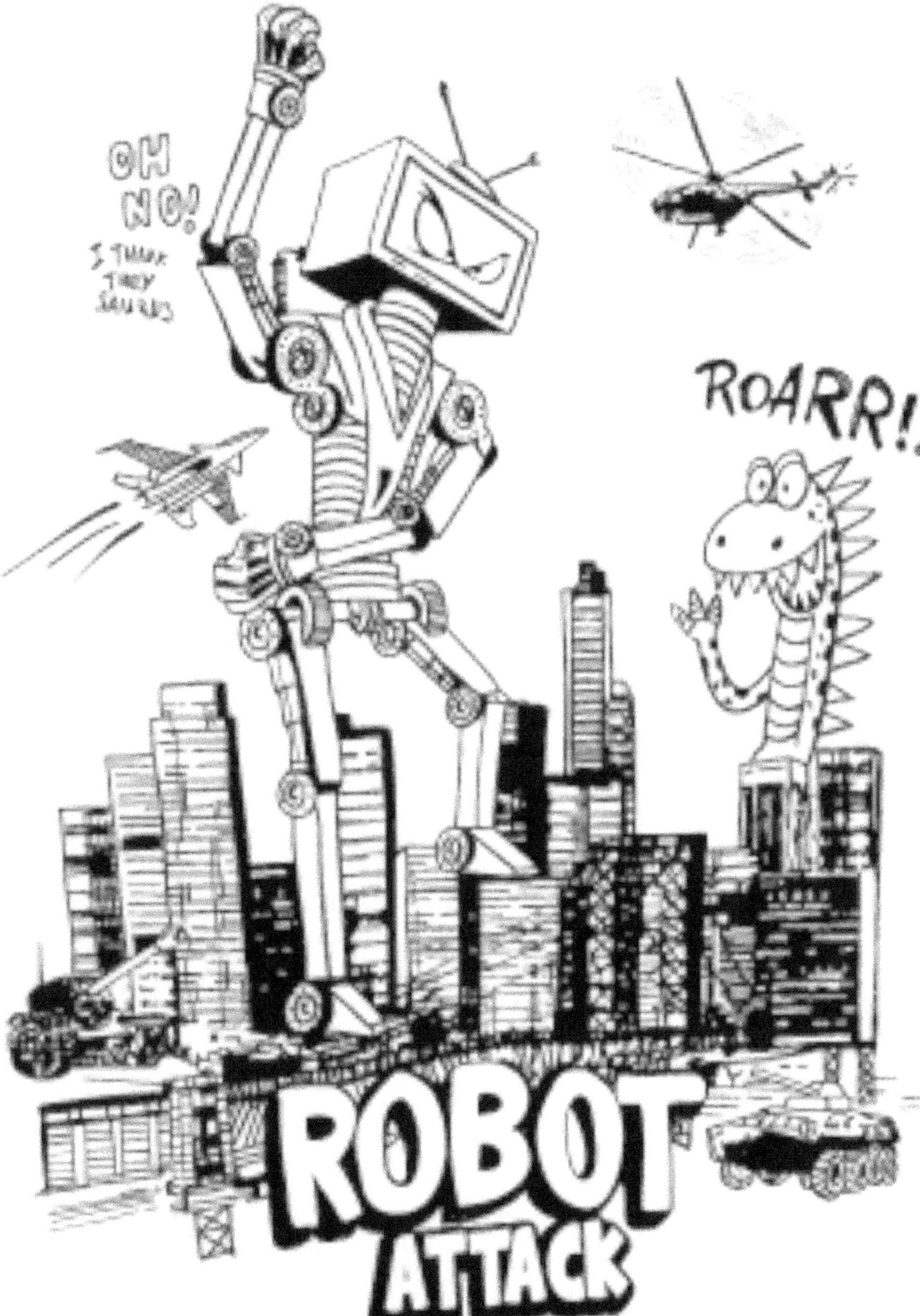
OH NO!
ROARR!!
ROBOT ATTACK

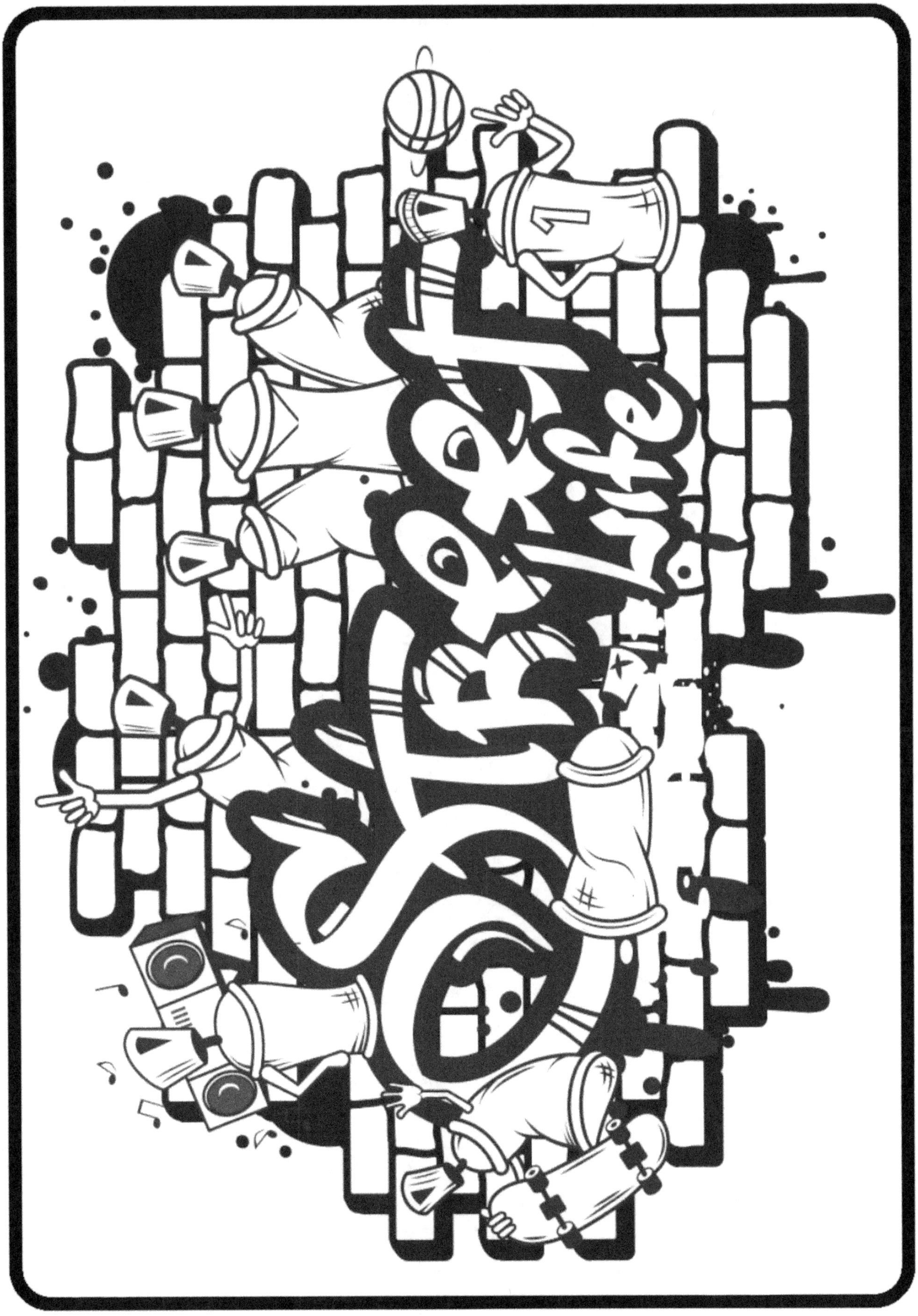
Street Life

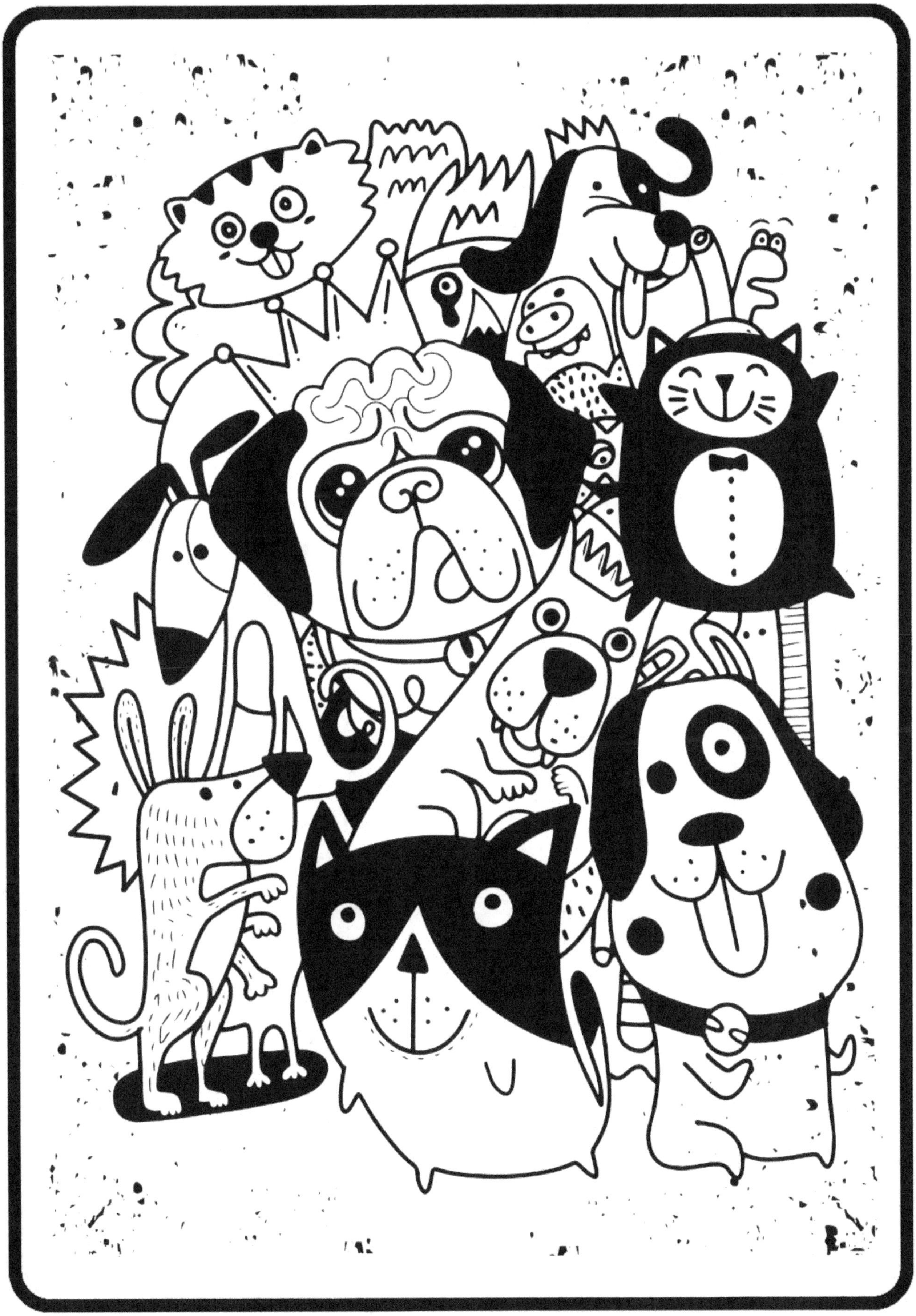

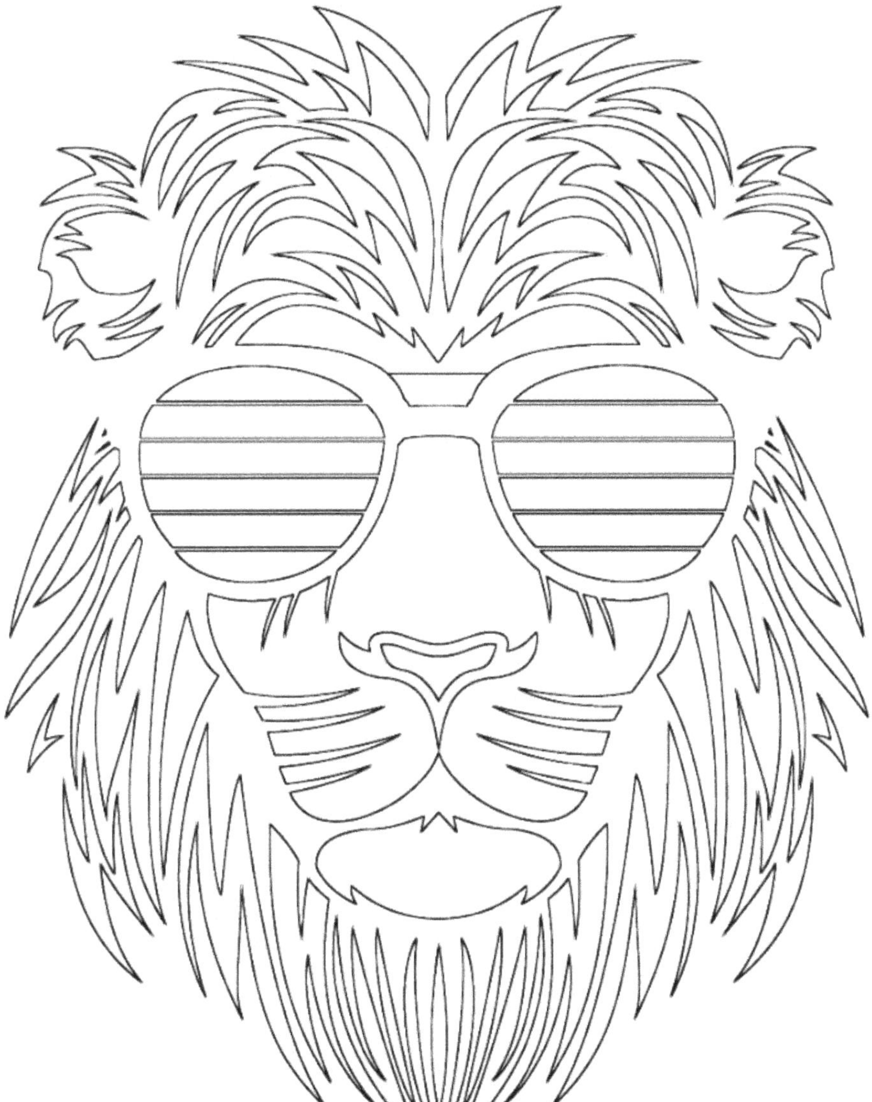

IT'S WAY TOO

PEOPLEY

Outside

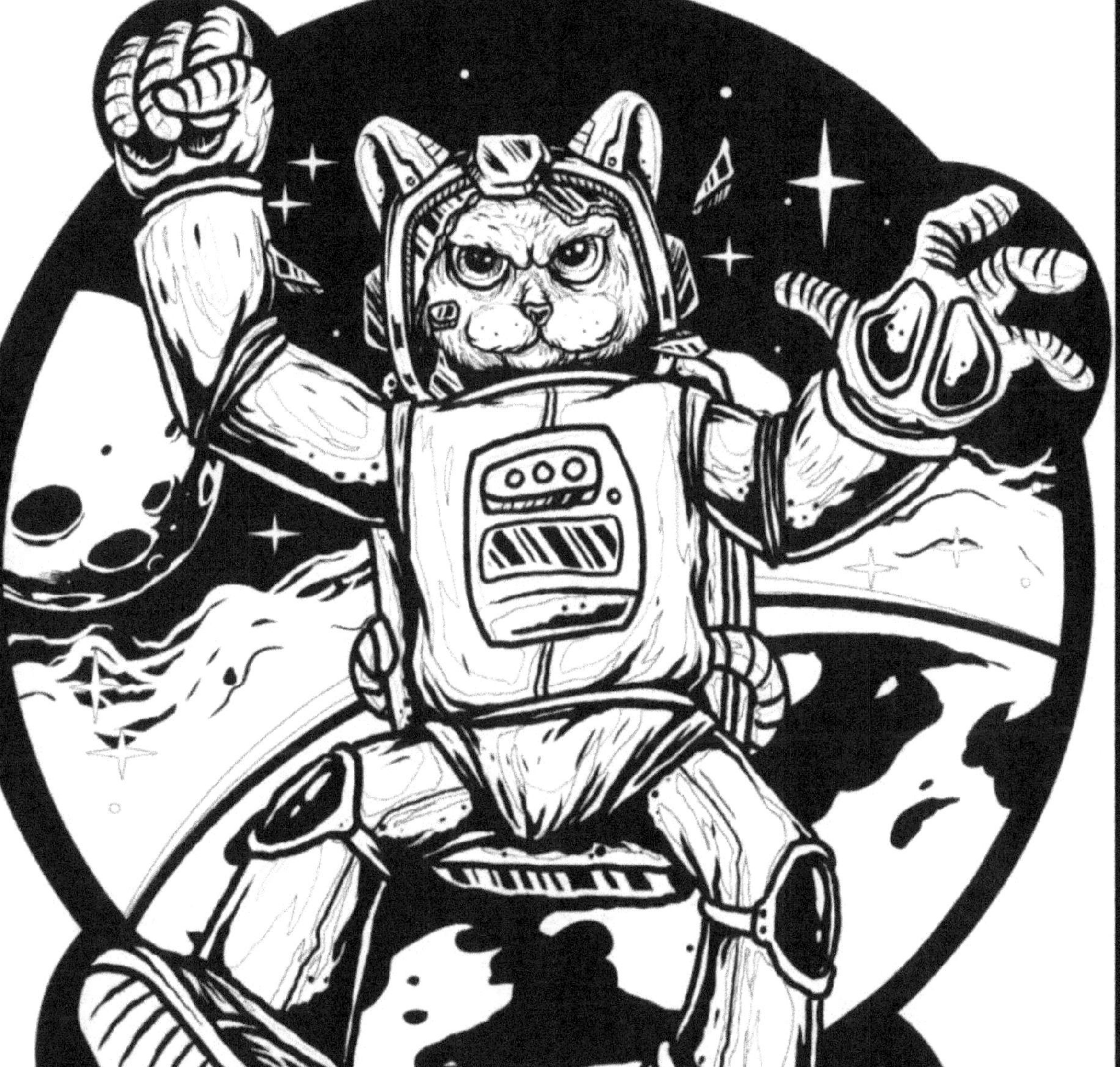

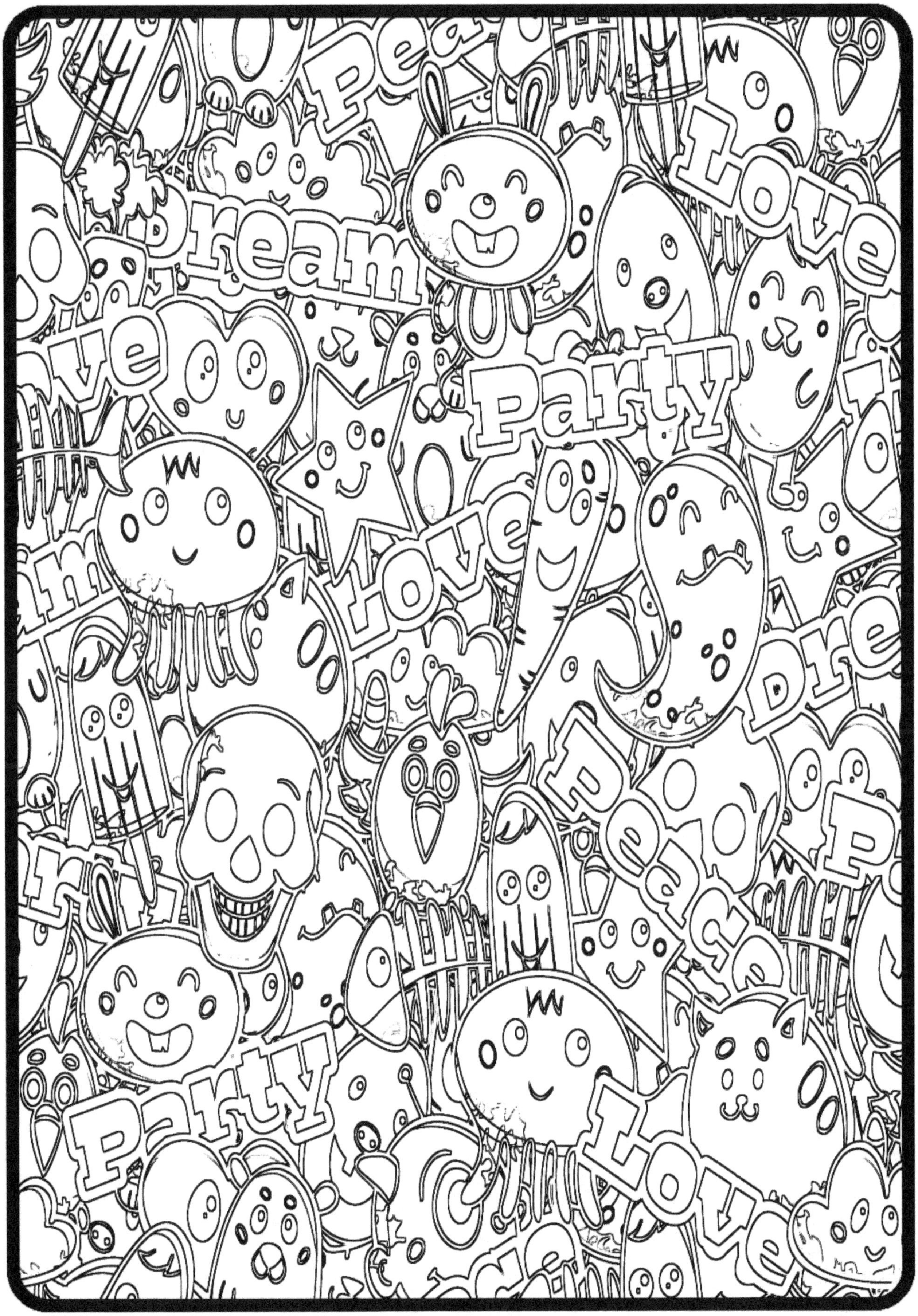
Love
Dream
Party
Love
Peace
Party
Love

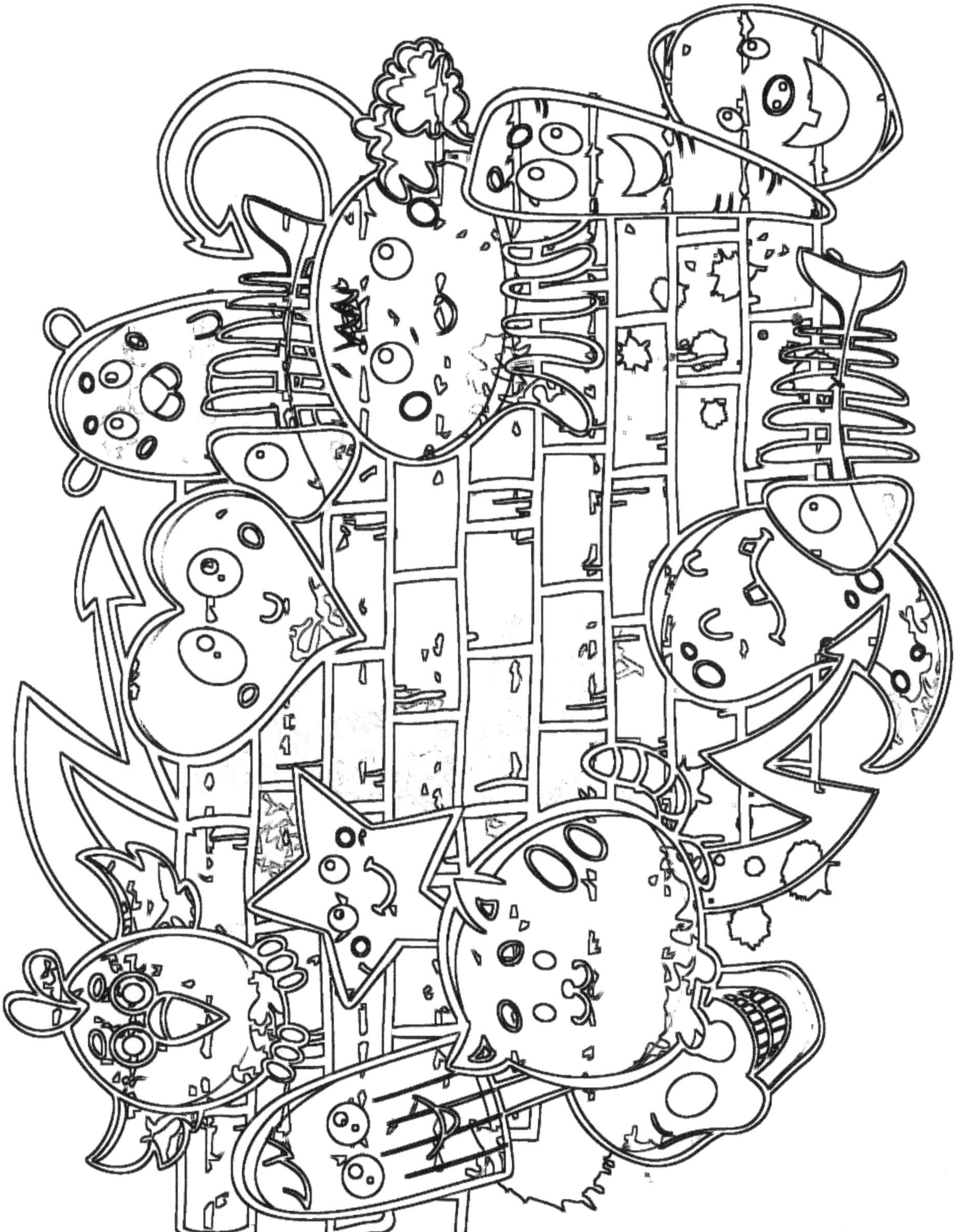

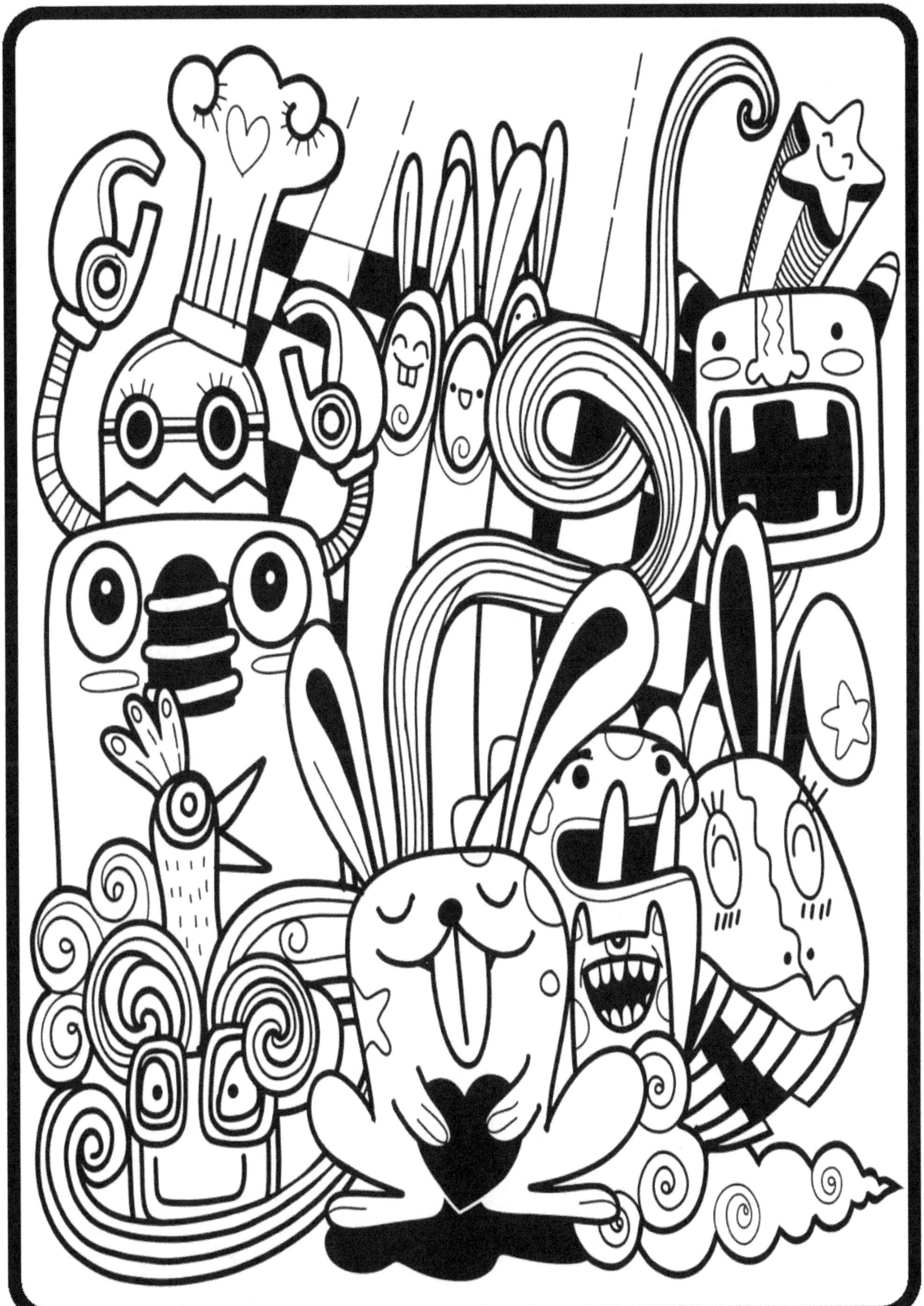

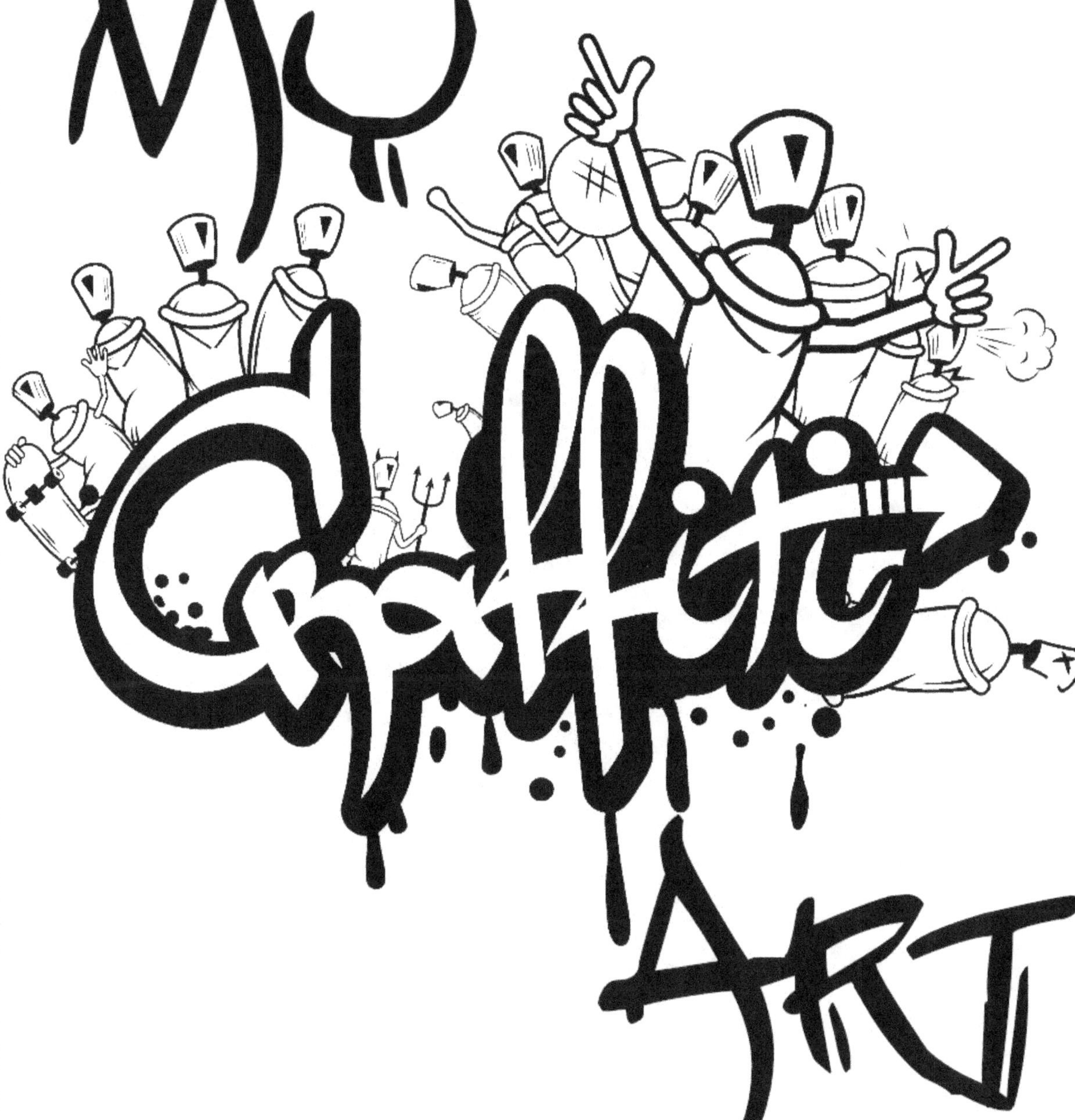
My Graffiti Art

www.ingramcontent.com/pod-product-compliance
Lightning Source LLC
Chambersburg PA
CBHW081011170526
45158CB00010B/2996